Runes Explained

Runic Guide for Beginners

Runes Overview, Runic Principles, History and Origin, Runic Symbols, Aetts, Casting Runes, Runic Gods and More!

By Riley Star

Foreword

The art of runes began in the time of Odin during the Viking period; it's the time when the Vikings did several military missions and sailed to the shores of Scandinavia. Odin in Norse mythology was the chief god, and his legendary horse called Sleipnir had runic symbols that are engraved in its teeth. Fast forward to present day, the story of Odin, the religion of runes, and runic alphabet was passed on and didn't die with the Vikings.

Many people of today aren't usually aware of the Vikings and their culture but thanks to the efforts of television shows and movies, we get to learn about their gods and also how they have lived in human history. However, only a few people still practice the Viking's runic "religion,"fortunately even if that's the case, wisdom is timeless and its source never dries up. Through the runic symbolism or alphabets that contains the timeless wisdom of our predecessors, you can use it to seek the answer to your questions and if done right, it can become a guide in your daily life. The questions shouldn't be about the future but more of the now – at the moment. It can also be a source of something profound that will involve a person's emotional or spiritual needs.

Runes is used to link an individual's logical mind and the unconscious/ sub – conscious which is why tapping into this ancient form can help you to increase your personal awareness and also guide you in your self – discovery. This book will introduce you to this ancient art and cover everything you need to know about its fascinating history, its principles, uses, rune alphabet, meanings, and how this ancient wisdom can be practiced and applied in one's daily life.

Table of Contents

Introduction to Runes

Runes are also known as *Futhorc, Futhark or Elder Futhark* after the six letters of the traditional order in the runic alphabet. The Runic Alphabet went through a lot of changes as time goes by, and these characters aren't only an alphabet during the Odin's time but it also has its own spiritual meaning. Just like the Hebrew and Egyptian ancient alphabets, the Runic Alphabet isn't just mere letters as each character or symbols correspond to certain meanings. Runic symbols also have some similarities to Germanic races, and other early languages like the Celtic. The interesting thing about it is that the ancient Vikings regarded these symbols as something magical and draw meaning from it. Later in this book you'll see the various letters of the Runic Alphabet which are usually written in straight lines, maybe because it's much easier to carve it on stone or surfaces. We'll also give a link of what the runic symbols stands for in the modern day English language in the next few chapters.

Facts and Meanings of Runes

Runes or runestones are words or symbols that have been found in the stones of Scandinavia and are believed to be used as a tool for self – help or self – awareness. Runes means mystery, magic, whisper or secret – and this perhaps is the main reason why the original meanings were never written down because it's meant to only be passed on by word of mouth or by someone who seeks for its wisdom just like the Kabbala language in Hebrew.

Today, such stones can be seen in the Stockholm Museum. Historians and anthropologists found a lot of original runic carvings all over Europe but only the ones carved in stone remains intact. As mentioned earlier, relatively a few people know about the runes and even fewer understood its meaning and significance. In 1960's though, the symbols became more accessible and attracted attention which is why it became quite known around the world, and some people started using it but because the original meanings were lost in time, modern day "rune masters" have to formulate new interpretations which heavily relies on their intuition just like how tarot card readers interpret the meanings of their tarot cards. According to the Vikings, it's not just a means of communication to oneself; it's also their way of talking to the gods so that they can be guided in their everyday lives.

Rune Masters

According to historians, the last great rune masters died around the 17th century in Iceland. They were priests and priestesses or otherwise known as the wise men and women who understand the meanings of the runic alphabet and its significance. Fortunately today, learning about the art of runes are now made commercially available and could breed the next rune masters. Hopefully after you read this book, you'll become more fascinated and curious with its principles and help you form a bridge between your conscious and subconscious and be able to draw meaning off of its ancient wisdom.

Chapter One: The History and Uses of Runes

Runes are used in various ways but today it's a tool that can help us understand more about ourselves, and enables us to tap in the energies within ourselves. There's nothing to fear because it is just a system and not some form of supernatural oracle or a cult that needs some form of sacrifice like what you mostly see on TV.

The runic alphabet is only meant to guide you through your journey to self – discovery and also serve as a tool to help you achieve self – development. The runes can function as both a tool and a teacher. In this chapter you'll get to know the brief history of runes as well as an introduction to its ancient and modern use.

Uses of Runes

According to ancient and modern - day rune masters, rune stones carry some form of strong healing energies in the form of vibrations that can help heal and protect the owner and also help them in their financial lives. One of the most important things to remember is that the art of runes is not a game or a toy therefore it should be taken seriously.

For those of you who have seen or read the book called Lord of the Rings, runes were suggested as implements of power, and in reality it is true since ancient Vikings regarded it as such. It has its own folklore and is a subject of mystery for some but it's something that should be respected not feared or even regarded as a joke. It should be cared for like how tarot readers or fortune tellers care for their cards or stones. You have to thank these powerful tools after using them and make sure that they are properly cared for so as not to lose its essence.

Runes can be used in different ways but mostly it is now used as a means of altering the current alphabet that we have in order to provide alternative lettering or even meanings of our names. You might often see it used as an amulet to provide the owner some sort of positive energy. The letters of the Runic Alphabet are often times used to change names for people who feel like their current name has some form of negative energy. Runic alphabet is also seen engraved in swords or shields during the early times for protection and also for healing. Rune stones or the runic alphabet can also be linked in numerology as the Vikings believed that the numbers 3 and 8 have certain magical powers.

Runic Links

Runes are known to be linked to other art forms like astrology and various elements such as earth, fire, water and air. It is also linked with the symbols of love. Some historians also think that the runic alphabet have some form of resemblance to Zodiac signs and glyphs of ancient Egypt. Rune stones can also correspond to the planets.

Aside from all of these, it is also known to have strong links to Tarot reading and I Ching (which is the polarity of symbols). The great thing about the art of runes is that even though it's an ancient system lost through time, the principles guiding it are not outmoded and it is as relevant today as it is during the ancient times. Aside from the alphabet, it's linked with systems of numerology and also color.

The image on the next page is the 18 rune system or the Elder Futhark.

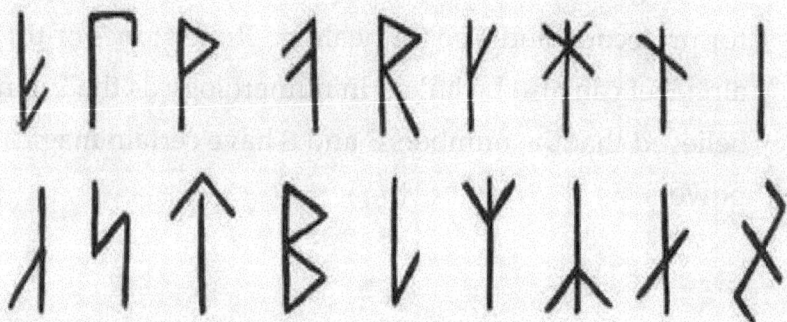

The Runic Alphabet and Its History

The Runic is a set of symbols and alphabet that are carved into objects like stones, woods, and caves for magical purposes. Some rune masters believe that the word "rune" came from the ancient German word called "raunen" that also has different meanings including 'to carve or cut.' Other rune practitioners suggest that the name is an Anglo – Saxon word called 'secgan' meaning 'to say,' others think it's a Latin word called 'secare' meaning 'to cut' still others suggest that it's from an Icelandic term 'runar' meaning 'whisper.'

When you look at the runic alphabet, you'll mostly notice that it is a series of straight lines that forms no ellipses or even curves which is quite obvious that it will fit the kind of intelligence level of the early man. During the ancient times, the only people who were taught to write or carve symbols are those who are rich or someone from a powerful family. One is considered educated if they know how to write and understand the alphabet and symbols.

Historians have various theories of where runes or runic alphabet originated. According to folklore, it is older than the New Testament or way before the time of Jesus Christ. It is linked with Odin, the one – eyed chief god, who is also known as one shape – shifter and was believed to have many disguises. It was believed that Odin gave up his eye as an offering to the gods, and in turn he was allowed to drink from the Fountain of Wisdom which is why he has abundant knowledge.

Odin came from an old Norse word which means 'spirit,' and is someone equivalent to the Greek god Hermes, Egyptian god called Thoth, and the Roman god Mercury.

The story of Odin has a strong runic connection because he is believed to be someone who wanted to understand life and death, and someone who thirst for knowledge. He wounded himself with his sword and impaled himself in a tree called Yggdrasil or commonly known in other alternative religion as Tree of the World. According to the story, Odin stayed under the tree of 9 days and 9 nights without basic necessities like food and water. He eventually found enlightenment, saw the stones, and carved the runic alphabet that 'came from the gods.' He wrote Poetic Edda that comprises about 39 poems. This story is often compared to the Tarot card illustration known as the 'Hanged Man.'

Practical Uses of Runes in Ancient History

One of the main uses of runes during the time of the Vikings is for protection and healing. The great thing is that it is still carried on in present time. The students of runes in present time usually carry stones with runic carvings whenever they go to say their doctor or if they need to visit someone at the hospital. It can be compared to a student carrying lucky gemstones or crystals if they wish to pass an examination.

Healing runes are also referred to as Lim runes. These are symbols that were carved in the leaves or bark of what is believed to be a 'healing' tree.

The table below is a list of healing runes or rune stones used to aid illnesses in different parts of the body.

This is only for your information but if you wish to try it, we don't see any reason why it shouldn't be tried out especially if you are someone interested in studying the art of runes. We do suggest though that you shouldn't abandon the prescribed medication of your doctor regardless of whether you're using rune stones, herbs, crystals or other similar magical materials.

Remember that these things can only help you in healing and perhaps creating a more positive energy vibe for your body and that it is only complementary and not an alternative. Runes in particular are mostly used for meditation so that it can help you heal of whatever it is that you're complaining physically. It's also best that you carry with you at all times a rune item and wear it like a jewelry or amulet so that it can reinforce its healing powers.

Healing Runes	Body Part
Fehu	Chest, Lungs and Respiratory ilnnesses
Thurisaz	Heart problems
Eihwaz	Eye problems
Uruz	Muscles and anything connected with physical strength

Raido	Legs and gluteal muscles
Gebo	Toxic poisoning
Laguz	Kidney problems
Ansuz	Mouth, teeth, throat, stuttering problems
Wunjo	Breathing problems
Hagalaz	Wounds, grazes, and cuts
Nauthiz	Arm or hand problems
Jera	Bowel or digestive illnesses
Berkana -	Fertility problems
Kaunaz	Cysts, ulcers, abscesses, boils and anything associated with fever
Sowelu	Burns or skin problems
Algiz	Mental illnesses, depression or anxiety, head – related problems
Teiwaz	Rheumatics, joint illnesses,

	arthritis
Isa	For any form of loss of feeling or sensation
Inguz	Problems associated with male reproductive system
Ehwaz	Back problems or anything associated it
Mannaz	Sprains, pulled tendons, particularly in the feet or ankles
Dagaz	Fear, distress, nervous problems, stress
Othila	Genetic problems or anything that is inherited
Perth	Anything associated with childbirth problems or sexual organs

Other Uses of Runes

As previously mentioned Vikings used rune stones for different reasons, back then when it was use for magical purposes it is called as Ram runes. Lim and Brun runes are also used for various magical purposes. Mai runes also known as speech runes are used to 'right wrongs,' while Sig runes are used to win competitions or win wars, it is usually carved in the warrior's sword and shield to bring good luck during battles.

Aside from these, runes are coupled with chants and singing especially during conception of a child, during child birth. Runes are also used to protect the newborn child, assign a rightful name, and somewhat guide the baby into the kind of path he/she will take.

Biarg runes are used to protect the baby and the mother during birth while Swart runes were used by the Vikings when one passes away to help the deceased spirit return to its ancestors.

Hug runes are used to attract attention, a lover, used for mental agility, and enchantment purposes. Runes were also used to help rune masters determine which herbs or potions to take.

Chapter Two: Runic Symbols and Keywords

This chapter will provide you an introduction of the runes collectively before we delve further into the details and interpretations of each rune. Runes are symbols that link man with his spirit or subconscious, and each rune has its own meanings and interpretations just like the meanings being represented by the Tarot cards. Before we discuss in the next chapters the purposes and meaning of each runes, we'll first teach you what kind of runes to buy and use.

What Runes to Purchase

Runes should be ideally made out of stone or wood just like what the Vikings use back then. However, there could also be other natural materials that present rune masters use as substitute such bones, slate, limestone. You can buy runes in New Age boutiques, gift shops or you can find some in antique stores, and have it delivered or shipped at your house. Before you purchase anything, its best that you look all the possible options and buy something that feels right to you or something that you'll be comfortable using. Try to use your intuition and 'feel' the runes before buying them. This is similar to Tarot card readers where they really use their intuition and feel the set of cards before buying them. Buy something that resonates with you.

How to Protect Your Runes

Just like crystals or gemstones, the runes should always be clean before and after you use it especially if you bought it from a commercial store or an open shop where lots of people touched it. The runes should ideally be washed with mineral or spring water, and properly dry it before you put it in its pouch (which should also be ideally made out of silk, leather, velvet or felt). Buy a pouch that has a drawstring made out of leather or a simple thong.

You can also try and make your own pouch or a container where you can place the runes you purchased. Some people use a box that's made out of wood. Many rune masters use casting clothes but it's more of a preference. The important thing is to make sure that the runes are safe, clean, and not damaged.

The Aetts

The Elder Futhark or Runes have 3 divisions. Each division has 8 runes, and has a total of 24 runes. The 25th rune should be blank and must be separated from the rest. This is quite similar to the Greek's alphabet into groups of 8 but divided into 3 divisions which reflect the 3 worlds of universe. These sets of runes are an Icelandic term known as Aett. The meanings included in it are linked with lineage, and the 8 directions. Aett is also similar to Airt which is a Scottish word, and Aird which is an Irish word, and its meaning is something related to the 8th horizon which is a means of direction. The number 8 is something powerful and significant to the Vikings because it is believed as a number assigned to the gods. The number 3 is also powerful for the Vikings. There are 3 sets of Aetts namely; the Freyr's Aett, Haegl's Aett, and Tyr's Aett.

It's also important to note that even if each runic set has its own god, the overall rules of the runes are still the chief god which is Odin.

The first set is called Freyr's Aett which represents growth, unfolding, and increase; the second set is called Haegl's Aett which is known to set the elements; and finally, the third set is Tyr Aett which is meant to bring courage in the face of adversity since Tyr is a warrior god. Each rune has its own assigned god which is something that you'll learn later on in this chapter including the corresponding planet or zodiac sign as well as other animal and natural associations.

Later on in this chapter, you'll also learn about the runes that are associated with the universal elements which are earth, fire, water and air.

It's also important to point out that the aetts are set out from left to right in a sequence with Freyr's Aett on the top row. What most rune masters do before using them or putting them away is to line up the runes and feel each imprint with their own personal energy before wrapping it up.

Language and Alphabetical Links

Each runic symbol represents a letter that can also be equivalent in the modern English alphabet we now have today. It can also be linked to Old English lettering, Icelandic symbols and also German and Norwegian letterings. It's not that important to know all the alphabetical links or language links but it will come in handy if you want to buy another set of runes so as to have a variety or personalize your own rune set or have some sort of historical interest.

In addition to the symbols of the different languages aforementioned, each rune also has its own name and may have a slightly different traditional order particularly the 23rd and the 24th rune as it could be sometimes interchanged. Germanic letterings correspond to the normally used rune symbol.

Runic Symbols

Runic symbols

Modern	Old English	Germanic	Norwegian	Icelandic
F	ᚠ	ᚠ	ᚠ	ᚠ
U or W	ᚢ	ᚢ	ᚢ	ᚢ
TH or P	ᚦ	ᚦ	ᚦ	ᚦ
A or O	ᚪ	ᚨ	ᚬ	ᚬ
R	ᚱ	ᚱ	ᚱ	ᚱ
K or C	ᚻ	ᚲ	ᚴ	ᚴ
G	ᚷ	ᚷ	-	-
W, U or V	ᚹ	ᚹ	-	-
H	ᚾ	ᚾ or ᚺ ᚼ	ᚼ	ᚼ

Modern	Old English	Germanic	Norwegian	Icelandic
N	ᚾ	ᚾ	ᚾ	ᚾ
I	ᛁ	ᛁ	ᛁ	ᛁ
J, G or Y	ᚼ	ᚼ	ᚼ	ᚼ
E, EO or EI	ᛃ	ᛃ	–	–
P	ᛈ	ᛈ	–	–
Z, E or Y	ᛉ	ᛉ	–	–
S	ᛋ	ᛋ	ᛋ	ᛋ
T	ᛏ	ᛏ	ᛏ	ᛏ
B	ᛒ	ᛒ	ᛒ	ᛒ
E	ᛖ	ᛖ	ᛖ	ᛖ
M	ᛗ	ᛗ	ᛦ	ᛦ
L	ᛚ	ᛚ	ᛚ	ᛚ
NG	ᛝ	ᛜ	–	–

Modern	Old English	Germanic	Norwegian	Icelandic
O or E	ᛟ	ᛟ	–	–
D	ᛞ	ᛞ	–	–
A	ᚪ	–	–	–
AE	ᚫ	–	–	–
Y	ᛠ	–	–	–
IO	ᛡ	–	–	–
EA	ᛠ	–	–	–
Y	–	–	ᛇ	ᛇ

Runic Names

English Letter	Old Englis Name	Germanic Name	Keywords
A, O	Os	Ansuz Asa	God Odin/ Holy Power
R	Rad	Raido	Travel/ Motion/ Wheel
K, C	Cen/ Cean	Kaunaz Kenaz Kano	Illumination/ Bonfire
G	Gyfu	Gebo	Partnership/ Gift
W,U, V	Wyn	Wunjo	Happiness/ Joy
H	Heagl	Hagalaz	Constraint/ Hail
N	Nyd	Nauthiz	Necessity/ Need
I	Is	Isa	Standstill/ Ice
J,G, Y	Ger	Jera	Cycle/ Year/ Harvest
E, EO, EI	Eoh	Eihwaz	Defence/ Yewtree
P	Peord	Perth	Womb/ Initiation

Z,E,Y	Eolh	Algiz	Guardianship/ Reed
S	Sigel	Sowelu	Life Force/ Sun
T	Tir	Teiwaz	Wargod
B	Beore	Berkana	Growth/ Birchtree
E	Eh	Ehwaz	Horse/ Movement
M	Man	Mannaz	Human Being
L	Lagu	Laguz	Fluidity/ Flow/ Lake
NG	Ing	Inguz	Energy/ Male Fertility
O, E	Epel/ Ethel	Othila	Home/ Inheritance
D	Daeg	Dagaz	Breakthrough/ Day
A	Ac	-	Oaktree
AE	Aesc	-	Ashtree
Y	Yr	-	Horn
IO	Iar/ Ior	-	Eel
EA	Ear	-	Grave/ Death

Elemental Links

Before we go and discuss the meanings of each runes or symbols on the next chapter, we'll also give you a brief background on how these runes are also linked with the universal elements. Most people especially those with background in astrology or zodiac signs are well aware of the universal elements namely; earth, fire, water and air. Just like in other magical systems or ancient alternative religions, runes and runic symbols also correspond to such elements.

Earth Element

The earth element is associated with anything solid and is mostly concerned with what's going on in reality. For instance, the rune called Eihwaz is an earth rune. The Eihwaz is also referred to as the 'Rune of Death' because it is linked with a yew tree which has poisonous qualities. Other runes that are linked with the earth element include Uruz, Othila, Isa, Wunjo, Jera and Berkana. In addition, Jera, Isa, and Eihwaz also have some links to the New Moon.

Water Element

Kaunaz rune is one example of a water rune and even though it is related to bonfires it doesn't equate as a fire element. Vikings regard bonfires as a representation of the physical light in the darkness. For them it also symbolizes enlightenment, emotions, inner knowledge and intuition which is why the element is water. However, some rune masters disagree to this and just kept Kaunaz associated with the fire element. Other runes that are linked with the water element include Lagu, Raido, Gebo, Perth, and Ing. Hagalaz rune is linked with ice which is why it's also appropriate for this element. In addition, Gebo, Raido, and Kaunaz also have some links to the Waning Moon. However, Raido and Gebo are also associated with the air element.

Air Element

An air rune called Ansuz is strongly connection with chief god Odin who was the one who discovered the runes in the Tree of the World. Vikings consider Odin as a source of language, inspiration and also knowledge, runes is his way of communication. The Ansuz rune is also related to the divine breath, to the intellectual power, and to the air element as well as to one's thoughts. In addition, Berkana, Ehwaz, and also Teiwaz also have some links to the Waxing

Moon. Algiz, Mannaz, and Sowelu are also part of the air element. However, some rune masters also suggest that Ansuz is more related to the water or fire element and not air.

Fire Element

Dagaz is an example of a fire rune and it's also related to the dawn of the world since it was believed that the earth is born in flames. The Dagaz rune is considered is something that can't be destroyed. It's also associated with light and the rune is said to be a source of illumination. It is a sort of protector and a guardian to harmful or destructive forces. However, the Dagaz rune is also associated with the air element which is why it is also known as an elemental duality.

In addition, Fehu and Othila are also under the fire element and have some links to the Full Moon and also with the earth element making it a form of elemental duality. Eihwaz, Thurisaz, and Nauthiz are also a fire element. It's important to note that the Eihwaz rune belongs to all four elements.

Chapter Three: The Runic Gods

If you wanted to become truly familiar with the runes and the art form, you should make sure that you have your own set of cards before going further. If you haven't found one to your liking yet or had no time to buy, you can perhaps make a temporary set of cards that will represent the runic symbols just so you can practice it until you finally get to have your own set of runes.

In the meantime, before we go further in explaining the meaning and possible interpretations of each rune in the next chapter, we'll first discuss with you the Runic Gods and Runic poetry because this will set out the foundation for what you're about to learn in the upcoming lessons. Being familiar with the Viking gods, their 'powers,' and the runic poetry will be helpful because runes are related to these specific gods.

The Runic Gods

According to the Vikings, there are 3 Norse gods namely; Odin, Freyr, and Thor. As you've learned earlier, Odin is known as the chief god but it wasn't always the case because evidence suggests that a god named Tyr (also known as Teiwaz, Tiwaz, Tiew, Ziu) was the original sky god or chief god. Tyr is known to be associated with his own rune which is why the 3rd aett is named after him. Tyr's name is also often seen etched in the jewelries and swords/shields/weapons of the warriors for their protection during war. In this section, we'll take a look at the different gods of the Vikings.

Tyr – The God of War

According to historians, Tyr was the Norse equivalent of the Roman god Zeus. Tyr is known as the god of war, and he is someone who is very brave and powerful. Odin apparently superseded Tyr.

Odin – The Chief God and Lord of the Slain

Odin was known as the god of mystery because he is always in disguise. However, he is more of a sinister figure, and commonly referred to as the Lord of the Slain. Another name for the chief god Odin is Thund along with around 170 other names according to the Anglo – Saxons. It is said that Odin has a palace in Asgard (equivalent of heaven) which is known as Valholl or the 'Hall of the Slain,' a place where fallen warriors go to after their death and prepare for their last battle known as the Ragnarok or the 'doom of the Gods.'

Creatures that have strong associations with Odin are the raven, wolf and eagle. According to legend, the wolf was said to guard the western door of Valholl while the eagle hovered on top. The ravens were Odin's secret spies that enable him to known what's happening in the world.

Chief god Odin is also known as the god of the dead, the warriors, war and magic and also as the patron of poetry. He is often depicted carrying a spear called Gungnir while riding with Sleipnir, his horse with 8 legs. He also wears a blue cloaked and a brimmed hat pulled over his one eye along with his ravens. He has a wife named Frigg, and 2 sons called Thor and Baldur.

His son Thor is more powerful and popular than his brother Baldur. He is depicted as someone who is huge, a red – hair with red beard, and always carrying his hammer called Mjolnir to protect the world. The hammer could be thrown or swung and goes back to Thor like a boomerang. This is exactly where Marvel Comic's 'Thor' film was based from.

Thor – The God of Thunder

As you know from the movies, Thor is the God of Thunder and the Lord Protector of the Universe because his powers have the elements of lightning and thunder. Thor is known to spend his time protecting Asgard and Midgard (the universe that man lives in) against forces and giants that are outside the limits of civilization.

The Vikings believe that whenever there's a storm, it means that Thor is moving around in the heavens with the thunder as the movement, and the lightning as him throwing his hammer and fighting off giants. Thor is also known as the god of seamen and farmers because he can provide a better weather through the wind and rain. He is depicted as someone who is noble, courageous, powerful and approachable both by gods and man alike especially in times of trouble.

There's a runic symbol that is said to represent Thor's hammer. Aside from his Mjolnir hammer, he also carries with him a pair of iron gauntlets and a magic belt. According to various theories, Thor was as significant as Odin during the time of the Vikings, and even more so because Thor's temple is always given the prime spot.

Freyr – The God of Peace, Fertility, and Good Fortune

Another important god to the Vikings is known as Freyr or Frey. He has a twin sister called Freya, and both of them are associated with the earth, seasons, and fertility. Freyr aside from being the god of fertility is also strongly linked with the seasons and weather especially the spring and summer.

Freyr is also known as the god of peace and good fortune. The most sacred animal that's associated with him is the wild boar, and in Swedish people still considers him as the most important god of all. According to legend, Freyr's most treasured possession is a ship built by dwarves known as Skiobladnir. The ship is big enough to carry all of the gods. Freyr's aett is dedicated to this god.

Other important Viking gods are the following:

- Njord – God of the Sea
- Heimdal – Guardian of the Bridge of Asgard
- Mordgud – Goddess of the Underworld
- Loki – God of the Underworld (brother of Odin)

Runic Meanings

Runes when casted out can have other spiritual meanings based on their traditional foundations. In the upcoming chapters you'll see how each rune is connected with the zodiac, animal/ nature, and planets. However, the astrological links we will give later on is based on modern thinking and not the original or traditional. We'll also quote some runic poems to give you further details on how the runes are also link with different Viking gods, polarity, colors, and also how it's connected with Thorsson's Tarot Card.

The runes will also have a different meaning if it's laid in an upright or reverse position which is also something that you'll learn later on. It is essential that whenever you make runic readings, you also consider any spiritual or intuitive meaning, and not just based on technicalities. Sometimes runes will call the reader or the practitioner to provide his/her own meaning, and even meditate on it so you can bring out any intuitive powers that can help you formulate your own interpretations. Hopefully as you delve deeper in learning about the meanings of each rune, you'll also gain personal meanings off of it but of course it will only come through experience and practice.

Runic Poetry

The rune's names usually follow the Germanic version or the Elder Futhark. It's important to note that the Icelandic and Norwegian runic poems are related to the sixteen runes that are used in the system unlike the Anglo – Saxon version poetry which covers around twenty – nine runes. For the next few chapters, we'll only be able to cover the 24 runes in the Germanic version, and also touch a bit on the 5 Anglo – Saxon rune verses.

Chapter Four: Freyr's Aett

In this chapter, we'll discuss the meanings and interpretations of various runes under the Freyr's aett including Fehu, Uyuz, Thurisaz, Ansuz, Raitho and Kaunaz. As what you've learned in the last chapter, Frey or Freyr is known as the god of peace, fertility, and good fortune. You'll also see the runic symbol of each as well as its corresponding relations to the zodiac sign, tarot card, color, and polarity. In addition, you'll also learn the relation of the runes to corresponding animals and nature as well as give you some lines from various versions of runic poems that a particular rune represents.

Fehu

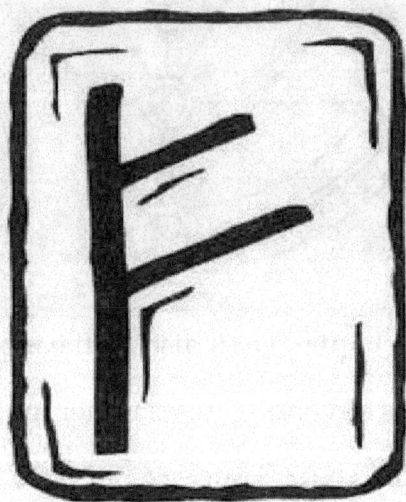

- Animal Relation: Cat
- Nature Relation: Elder Tree, Nettle
- Zodiac Sign - Taurus
- Tarot Link - The Tower
- Colour – Red
- Polarity – Female

- Anglo - Saxon runic poem in relation to Fehu: 'Feoh is comfort to all men, yet must everyman bestow it freely, if he wish to gain honour in the sight of the Great One.'

- Norwegian runic poem in relation to Fehu: 'Fe causes trouble among kinsmen; wolf dwells in forest.'

-

- The Icelandic runic poem in relation to Fehu: 'Fe is trouble among kinsmen and fire of sea and path of serpent.'

The god that is associated with the Fehu rune is Freyr or Freyja. Fehu means possessions; during the time of the Vikings, owning a cattle signifies that one is wealthy, has money, or it is something equivalent to success. The rune is regarded as a symbol of status and it implies that a person has some form of power or authority and is in a position to negotiate for a better deal if he/she chooses to.

In today's world, this kind of scenario still exists particularly among many countries in the African continent. Possessions are something that can be acquired, purchased, inherited or exchanged. It doesn't necessarily need to come as a result of hard work because sometimes it is simply passed on from one person to the next if he/she is worthy to have it. One should remember that possessions should be something to take care of and looked after. It has an element of conservation; you can make lots of money but keeping it and perhaps using it in the right way is also important. The rune poems that's related to Fehu warns the people to not be envious or greedy when it comes to wealth. This rune calls a person to protect and care for their possessions/ treasures. It's something that's also associated with a potential to have wealth and the need to consider sharing it with other people as some form of social responsibility.

Aside from fortune, Fehu is also associated with well – being, nourishment, and also fertility. It also tells us that we need to cooperate so that we can learn how to control our lives and our situations. According to rune masters, since Frey is the god of fertility, this rune can also be linked with love and pregnancy but it can also mean a start of something new.

In Reverse

If the rune of Fehu is laid in a reverse position then that could mean that some valuable thing is loss. It could be a material thing and also a loved one or loss of a certain relationship. It may also denote that there are problems when it comes to being fertile, and also lack of creativity or passion.

Uruz

- Animal Relation: Wild Ox/ Viking Oxen (Aurochs)
- Nature Relation: Birch tree; Icelandic moss
- Planet – Pluto
- Tarot Link - The High Priestess
- Colour - Green
- Polarity – Male

- Anglo - Saxon runic poem in relation to Uruz: 'Ur is proud and has great horns. It is a courageous beast and fights with its horns, a great ranger of moors, it is a creature of mettle.'

- Norwegian runic poem in relation to Uruz: 'Ur come from poor iron; reindeer runs oft over hard-frozen snow.'

- The Icelandic runic poem in relation to Uruz: 'Ur is weeping of clouds and destruction of hay-harvest and abhorrence of herdsmen.'

The Uruz rune is associated with Auroch or a Viking oxen/ wild ox is believe to be a very strong and powerful creature. However, it had been extinct since the 17th century.

The auroch possess sharp and long horns which is why 'the horn of plenty' has been established. These creatures moves very fast and is also capable of carrying loads and used as transportation.

The rune of Uruz therefore denotes that there may be a burden that's placed in one's shoulders with which one will be able to overcome or needs to overcome. The god is associated with Thor, the god of thunder.

Oxen represent physical strength, power and opportunities which is why it's essentially masculine in nature; it also represents an unlimited power in us. However, any strong creature like an auroch should never be pushed because since it's a source of power or has a naturally strong energy, one should be careful as to how much force should be exerted.

The rune of Uruz is also linked with harnessing energy and using it to achieve a favorable result to the one who uses it. If this rune is drawn, then that could mean that there'll be changes ahead but it is still up to the person to seize such ensuing changes. Usually, change brings some sort of uncertainties or 'fear of the unknown,' and sometimes one should be courageous enough to take risks, practice patience, and also not give up since as what they say, 'change doesn't happen overnight' because it's a process not an outcome. If ever you or your subject draws out this rune, and you're expecting something like an advancement or promotion then this is a good sign.

It is also worth noting that since auroch are what Vikings offer as a sacrifice, it could mean that before one can achieve any form of result, sacrifice might be required.

In Reverse

If the Uruz is laid in reverse then that means one can miss a change of in his/her life. The link with strength may also denote that there could be a form of illness, mental weakness or even lack of strength which is why it is essential that if you draw out a reverse Uruz, you should take the time to look at your health and make the necessary adjustments.

Thurisaz

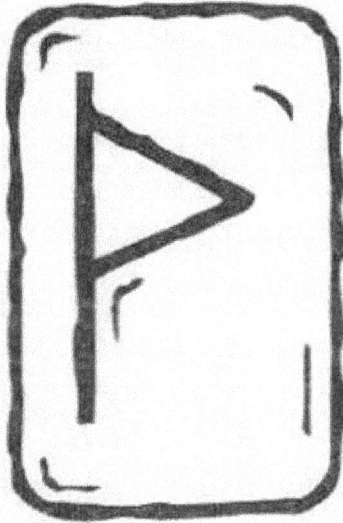

- Animal Relation: Snake; Blackthorn
- Nature Relation: Rose; thorn of bush; houseleek
- Planet – Jupiter
- Tarot Link - The Emperor
- Colour – Red
- Polarity – Male

- Anglo - Saxon runic poem in relation to Thurisaz: 'Thorn is exceeding sharp, a baneful thing for a warrior to touch, uncommonly severe on all who lie amongst them.'

- Norwegian runic poem in relation to Thurisaz: 'Purs causes illness in women; few rejoice at ill luck.'

- The Icelandic runic poem in relation to Thurisaz: 'Purs is illness of women and cliff dweller and husband of Varthrun.'

The rune has strong links with an aggressive nature and also with Thor. And it is therefore connected with defense, aggression, conflict or standing one's ground. During the time of the Vikings, they use thickets of blackthorn or hawthorn were use as boundaries to keep out intruders. When reading the Thurisaz rune it's important to note this defensive connection. The problems are something that could be minor but also worrisome though it is something that can be overcome in time.

The rune denotes that now is not the time to make risky decisions because change can come without any warning. Perhaps this is also the time to let go of the past, look what you have achieved, and also the things you are looking forward to.

It can denote that people may not be as reliable as you think just like the rose - that even if it looks beautiful there could still be a thorn that can harm you.

The Thurisaz rune also suggests that one should take precaution in doing business deals at this time. There could also be rivalries in business, and also choices that needed to be determined in the family. This rune suggests self – protection, but also unexpected luck. It is connected with Thor's day and could also be a call for your to challenge your opponents just like the god of thunder but in a defensive position.

In Reverse

If the Thurisaz is laid in reverse then it could mean that one should act in haste. Patience should be practiced because repent at leisure is what the reverse rune suggests. Tensions may also be high.

Ansuz

- Animal Relation: Wolf; Raven; Fly Agaric Toadstool
- Nature Relation: Ash Tree
- Planet – Mercury (negative phase)
- Tarot Link - Death
- Colour – Dark Blue
- Polarity – Male

- Anglo - Saxon runic poem in relation to Ansuz: 'Os is the source of all language, a pillar of wisdom and a comfort to the wise, a blessing to warriors.'

- Norwegian runic poem in relation to Ansuz: 'Oss is source of most travel; but scabbard is of swords.'

- The Icelandic runic poem in relation to Ansuz: 'Oss is ancient creator and king of Asgard and lord of Valholl.'

As what you've learned in the previous chapter, the chief god Odin is usually depicted with ravens. Drawing out the rune of Ansuz symbolizes Odin's protection; it is also known as the "God Rune." The rune is also related with The Ash Tree/ Tree of the World known as Yggdrasil.

It could mean that Odin is teaching a person based on his knowledge of language, and personality. It is also linked with spoken word, learning, scholarship, communication, and people that achieved a high status. It denotes that a certain person who is wiser than us can perhaps give us advice, mentor us or just give a moral support; it could also be likened to a father figure since Odin is considered as the Fatherly god.

In Tarot, the rune of Ansuz is also associated with The Emperor and The Hierophant despite its linked with the Death card.

Odin is known to have the ability to change shape/ guises at will which is why if one draws out this rune, it can also mean that a certain circumstance can quickly change at any given moment. One should also take note of their dreams as it can serve as a guide if this rune is picked.

In Reverse

If the Ansuz is laid in reverse, it could denote that problems are likely to arise with older people. It also suggests that there are problems with communication, with studies, or even wasted efforts. It can also denote a problem with the throat or anything related with communication; travel time could also be halted.

Raido

RAIDO

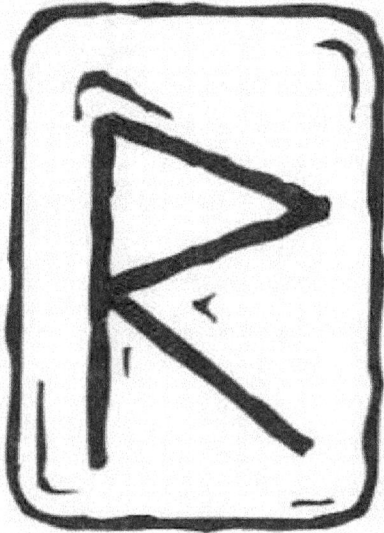

- Animal Relation: Goat
- Nature Relation: Mugworth; Oak Tree
- Zodiac Sign - Gemini
- Tarot Link - The Hierophant
- Colour – Red
- Polarity – Male

- Anglo - Saxon runic poem in relation to Raido: 'Rad is easy for the warrior while he is indoors, and very courageous to him who travels the high road upon a stout horse.'

- Norwegian runic poem in relation to Raido: 'Raid is said to be worst for horses; Regin forged the best sword.'

- The Icelandic runic poem in relation to Raido: 'Reid is joy of rider and speedy journey and labouring of horse.'

The rune of raido is related to a god of called Ing. The main keywords for raido include ride, travel, journey, and cartwheel.

This rune represents a journey internally and externally speaking. It also denotes that one must have enough courage because it also indicates that the journey is not easy but in the end it will be worth it and rewarding.

The rune of raido also suggest that a person might be looking for means of transport so that one can go further into his/her own journey, perhaps an opportunity or a 'break' to help one to move upward or forward.

Raido is therefore a rune of movement, transport or travel, and action. It may be connected to legal matters, moving from one place to another or other important matters that goes in twos.

It also denotes that one should take note of anything that has 2 sides to it particularly in the aspect of communication. This is the time to reflect and take a look at one's spiritual journey or one's direction in life, and consider if a change in lifestyle is necessary. This could also an indicator that a person should use their own inner compass to guide them in making decisions that will take their life to new, and perhaps, better direction.

The rune of raido is also associated with the seasons of cycle whereby one can definitely experience some form of transformation, and indicates that situations are unlikely to remain stagnant.

In Reverse

When the rune of raido is laid in reverse could mean that things will not go according to plan. You or your subject will probably mess up the plans in place, or there could be unexpected things that will come up that will cause disruption in the journey. It could also mean that journeys might be aborted, and one can also find that they lack imagination.

Kaunuz

KAUNAZ

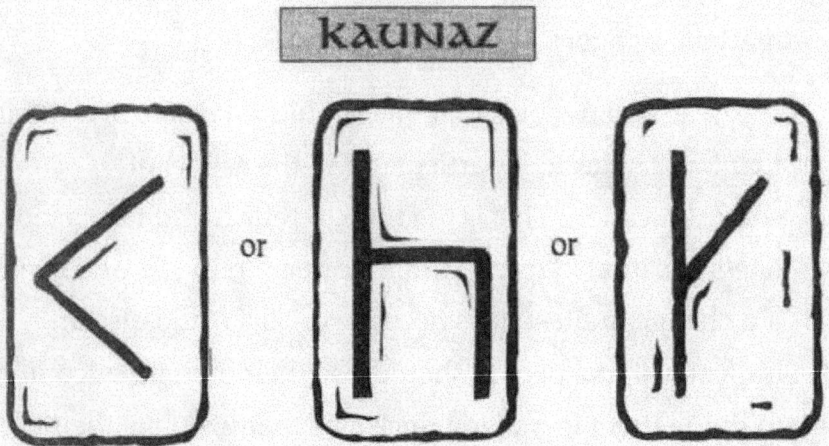

- Animal Relation: Night owl
- Nature Relation: Cowslip; Pine Tree
- Zodiac Sign - Aries
- Tarot Link - The Chariot
- Colour – Flame Red
- Polarity – Female

- Anglo - Saxon runic poem in relation to Kaunuz: 'Cen is known to all by its pale bright flame; it always burns where princes sit within.'

- Norwegian runic poem in relation to Kaunuz: 'Kaun is fatal to children; death makes a corpse pale.'

- The Icelandic runic poem in relation to Kaunuz: 'Kaun is fatal to children and painful spot and dwelling of putrefaction.'

The rune of kaunuz is related to a god of called Heimdall. The main keywords for this rune include mystery, female influence, and hope. It's also associated with positivity, new energy, and understanding.

If a woman draws this rune, it could denote that she will receive a man's love, and if a man draws this rune then it denotes that he will give joy to a woman. Therefore this rune can also be related to sexuality of a person.

The rune of Kaunuz is also linked with bonfire and because of this; it denotes bright flames of passion and also kindling a relationship.

It also denotes a form of psychic energy, knowledge, and insight that can come from within suggesting an inner light of knowledge. Therefore, it can suggest that other ideas, theories or knowledge can be superseded or replaced by the new idea or insight that is formed. It can also denote that there will be life after death, or regeneration from death.

During the time of the Vikings, fire is the element that protected them from the wild animals aside from the fact that it provides them warmth during cold days, and also cooks their food. In the same way, the rune of kaunuz can give protection or even create a new material just like how fire can be made by rubbing two objects.

This rune denotes success, guidance, protection, and support especially in the field of art. If one draws this rune it could mean that a person is on the right track and success will eventually come to them.

In Reverse

If the rune of kaunuz is laid in a reverse position then it could indicate loss of partner or friendship, and also possession. It could also bring possibilities of feeling ill, or some sort of unpleasantness in one's life.

It can also signify that one should perhaps replace old materials, and also a fading friendship so that a new relationship can be made or new things can be acquired.

It can also denote that a person feels that he/she is lost in life or has no direction, and unable to find someone or something by which to be guided.

Gebo

- Animal Relation: Oxen
- Nature Relation: Ash; Wych Elm Trees
- Zodiac Sign - Libra
- Tarot Link – The Lovers
- Colour – Royal Blue
- Polarity – Male and Female
- Anglo - Saxon runic poem in relation to Gebo: 'Gyfu brings credit and honour which support one's dignity,

it furnishes help and subsistence to all broken men, devoid of aught else.'

The rune of Gebo is associated with Gefn which is known as the god of abundance. The keywords for this rune include generosity, love, gift, and partnership.

It also denotes that peace will be the reward if one helps someone genuinely. The help that should be given may require some form of personal sacrifice and shouldn't be refused. Therefore this rune suggests that there should be self – sacrifice so that when the time comes that you're the one who needs help, help will come to you unexpectedly.

This is a good rune to draw if a person is working for some kind of charitable organization or for a particular cause. The rune of gebo can also mean finding love or starting a new romantic relationship. According to rune masters this rune signifies people joining together and cooperating for the common good. It has no meaning if it is drawn in a reversed position.

Chapter Five: Haegl's Aett

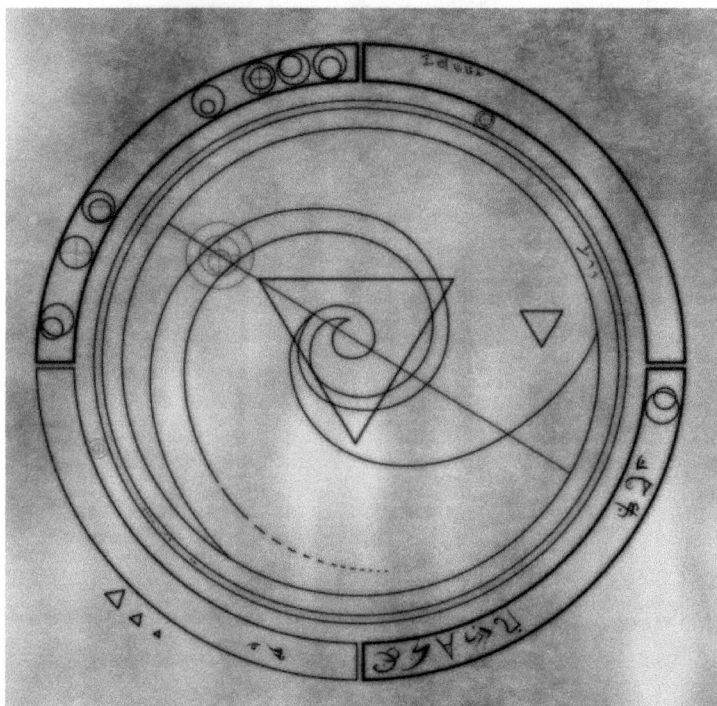

In this chapter, we'll discuss the meanings and interpretations of various runes under the Heagl's aett including Hagalaz, Nauthiz, Isa, Jera, and Eihwaz. You'll also see the runic symbol of each as well as its corresponding relations to the zodiac sign, tarot card, color, and polarity. In addition, you'll also learn the relation of the runes to corresponding animals and nature as well as give you some lines from various versions of runic poems that a particular rune represents. Do take note that some runes do not have a reverse meaning or it doesn't have any poem in certain poetry particularly in the Norwegian and Icelandic runic poem.

Hagalaz

ƕagalaz

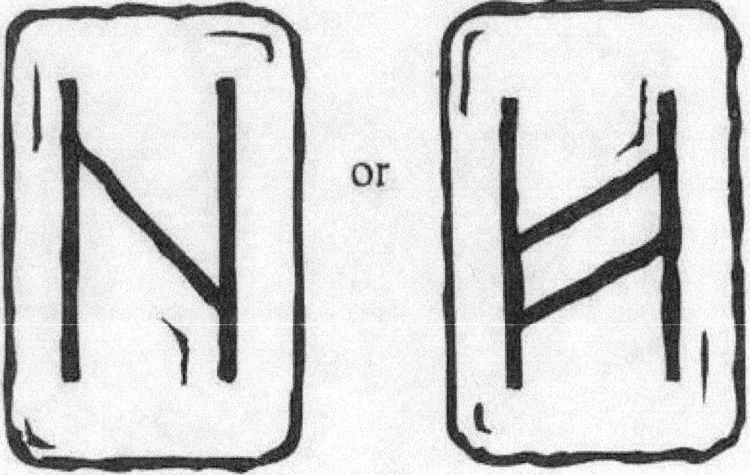

or

- Animal Relation: No direct animal relation
- Nature Relation: Ash Tree; Hawthorn; Yew
- Planet – Uranus
- Tarot Link – The World
- Colour –Blue
- Polarity – Female

- Anglo - Saxon runic poem in relation to Hagalaz:
  'Hagal is the whitest of grain, it is whirled from the
  vault ofheaven and tossed about by gusts of wind and
  then melts into water.'

- Norwegian runic poem in relation to Hagalaz: 'Hagall is the coldest of grains; Christ created the primaeval world.'

- The Icelandic runic poem in relation to Hagalaz: 'Hagall is cold grain and driving sleet and sickness of serpents.'

The rune of Hagalaz is linked to hail, sleet, and also icy conditions or winter. It's also related to an herb known as bryony.

Heimdall, is the name of the god that's associated with this rune; he is a watchergod and someone who is the gatekeeper of the bridge leading to the underworld.

Drawing the rune of Hagalaz may denote that there's some form of disruption, unforeseen events, and other elemental forces that could cause something to be delayed. It indicates that some unexpected things will occur or in a sudden manner, and that nothing can be done because it is out of one's control or influences. Therefore, this can be a chance for an individual learn or grow from whatever experience change will bring into their lives as it is sometimes necessary.

Also known as the rune of the gambler, Hagalaz may also denote that things might not turn out as planned but it can somehow mean that risks could be taken. In numerology, the Hagalaz rune is strongly linked with the number 9. And since this rune is related to winter, it brings a promise that whatever will happen is only temporary, and that it could bring forth the foundation to better things or spring time.

In Reverse

The Hagalaz rune may denote accidents if it's drawn in reverse but for some rune masters they believe that there's no meaning if it is laid in a reverse position.

Nauthiz

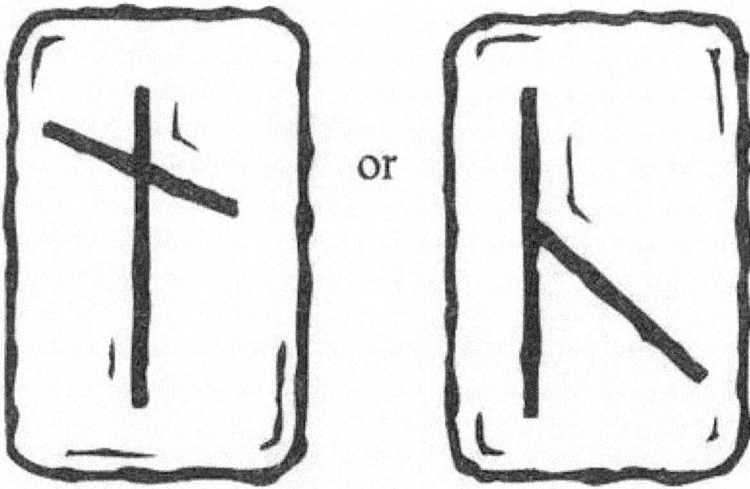

- Animal Relation: No direct animal relation
- Nature Relation: Rowan tree, mountain ash, beach
- Planet – Saturn
- Tarot Link – Devil
- Colour –Black
- Polarity – Female
- Anglo - Saxon runic poem in relation to Nauthiz:
  'Nyd is oppressive to the heart, yet often it proves a
  source of help and salvation to the children of men
  who heed it betimes.'

- Norwegian runic poem in relation to Nauthiz: 'Naudr leaves little choice; naked man is chilled by frost.'

- The Icelandic runic poem in relation to Nauthiz: 'Naud is distress of slave and state of oppression and hard labour.'

The Nauthiz rune is linked with a god known as Skuld, goddess Nott, and also Argonauts

Drawing the rune of Nauthiz suggests that one should think before doing anything. It also suggests that before making any decisions, one must know thyself and be clear of the reason why one will do such things; clarity of mind at this point is not at its best which is why the rune might be suggesting to take the time to really make any life – changing decisions especially if it's something related to a job or money.

The rune of Nauthiz also denotes that relationships could be strained at this point, and emotions could run high. It is best to understand one's limitations and become more patient when handling things. Such limitation doesn't only mean restrictions but perhaps boundaries. Do remember that things could change but plans shouldn't be totally abandoned. Being aware of oneself will help a person to not do anything they will later regret because it can also affect other people especially members of the family.

This rune is also use when a person is seeking protection from mental illness or psychic attacks.

In Reverse

If it is drawn in reverse denotes that a certain risk is taken but the result of it may still be unknown. It may also indicate feelings stress, tensions, or frustrations. Avoid 'get rich quick schemes' if this rune is drawn in reverse.

Isa

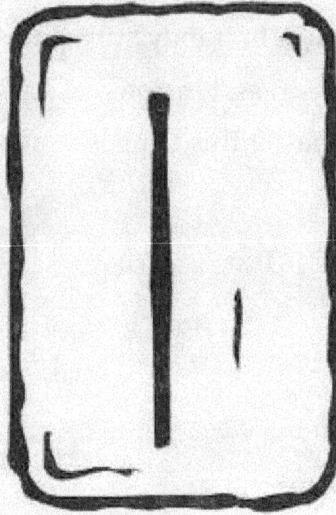

- Animal Relation: Reindeer; Wild Boar
- Nature Relation: Alder Tree; Herb Henbane; Iron
- Planet – Neptune
- Tarot Link – Hermit
- Colour –Black
- Polarity – Female
- Anglo - Saxon runic poem in relation to Isa: 'Is is very cold and immeasurably slippery, it glistens clear as glass and is most like to gems. It is a floor wrought by the frost, a fair sight.' heed it betimes.'

- Norwegian runic poem in relation to Isa: 'Is we call broad bridge: blind man must be led.'

- The Icelandic runic poem in relation to Isa: 'Iss is bark of rivers and roof of wave and destruction for doomed men.'

The rune of Isa is associated with a god called Verdandi, and it's strongly ice, and since ice is solidified water, it will eventually return to water but of course it will take some time. Therefore this rune denotes that patience is needed at this time.

It could also denote that there could be some emotional cooling especially in a relationship both romantic and in business. It could also denote separation or a pause in a relationship. However, this could also mean that the situation is only short – lived. The rune of isa in numerology is also linked with the number 7.

This can also mean that the money being expected will be delayed or completely not come at all. It also suggests that instead of pushing for a solution, it might be best to just leave it be because things will move naturally and it could also be an opportunity to have a change of plans.

Don't worry though because it also gives hope that just like how the ice will eventually melt, a situation may also eventually improve but of course it will take some time, which is why it's advisable to be patient, and learn to enjoy the process.

In Reverse

According to rune masters, drawing the rune of Isa in reverse position doesn't have any meaning since if the symbol is laid in reverse it still looks the same. Some people however suggest that the reverse rune can mean immobility or may denote a physical problem that will hinder a person to move from one place to another.

Jera

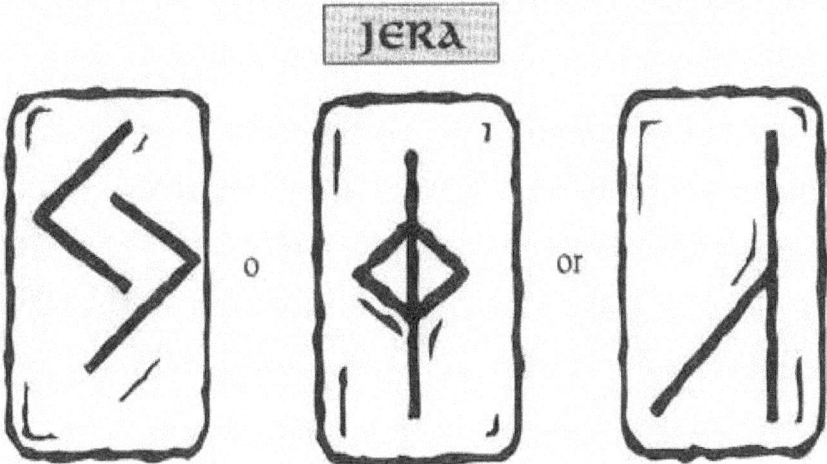

- Animal Relation: Reindeer; Wild Boar
- Nature Relation: Alder Tree; Herb Henbane; Iron
- Zodiac Sign: Virgo
- Planet – Neptune
- Tarot Link – The Fool
- Colour –Blue
- Polarity – Male/ Female
- Anglo - Saxon runic poem in relation to Jera: 'Jer is a joy to men when the Gods make the earth to bring forth shining fruits for rich and poor alike.'

- Norwegian runic poem in relation to Jera: 'Ar is a boon to men; I say Frothi was liberal.'

- The Icelandic runic poem in relation to Jera:
'Ar is blessing to men and good summer and fully
ripe crops.'

The rune of Jera is associated with Freyr, which is
why the keywords link to it is something related to fertility,
harvest, crop cultivation, reaping, and also good fortune as
reward from past efforts. Of course do remember the saying
that 'whatever you sow, you will reap.' If you didn't plant
anything, you won't harvest anything. It also denotes
completion, and full cycle.

This rune also indicates law and order or natural flow
of things. It could mean that one will be successful in
whatever endeavor is currently taken, and hope runs high. It
could mean that there'll be new projects that will come, a
new contract or client or even a new house.

Since the rune of Jera is connected with the full cycle,
this can mean that success or good fortune will come in the
next 12 months as this rune being the 12th rune. However,
this can also indicate that things will come to fruition but
luck may only last for a period of time specifically for a year.
It's a good rune to draw if one is looking for a fresh start
because it indicates an ending a new beginning.

In Reverse

Similar to the rune of Isa, the rune of Jera also look exactly the same when it is upside down which is why rune masters also believe that it doesn't have any reverse meanings.

Eihwaz

- Animal Relation: Horse
- Nature Relation: Bryony herb; apple tree; yew tree
- Zodiac Sign: Sagittarius

- Planet – Neptune
- Tarot Link – The Hanged Man
- Colour – Dark Blue
- Polarity – Male
- Anglo - Saxon runic poem in relation to Eihwaz: 'Eoh is a tree with rough bark, hard and fast in the earth, supported by its roots, a herder of fire and a joy upon an estate.'

The rune of Eihwaz is associated with the hunter god known as Ullr.

Even though its polarity is male, this rune portrays a powerful woman who can both bring good things or do something ill. Changes are also denoted but it may not be welcomed, and perhaps it should be best live for the moment.

The rune is also linked to the yew tree which can represent longevity and also continuity even after one's passing.

It also represents some form of progress or movement since it is linked with a horse. Business matters should be planned, and also have an optimistic outlook of the present and future.

Hardships even though it is expected may not actually come, and if there are any delays it will only be temporary but patience is also needed so that one can move in the right path. A person may not feel comfortable while waiting which is why flexibility and the ability to adapt is needed in every situation but you can look forward to things working out in your favor.

In Reverse

According to rune masters it's also one of the runes that doesn't have a meaning or negative indication if it's drawn in reverse. However, some people say that it could suggest a form of escapism or withdrawal.

Chapter Six: Tyr's Aett

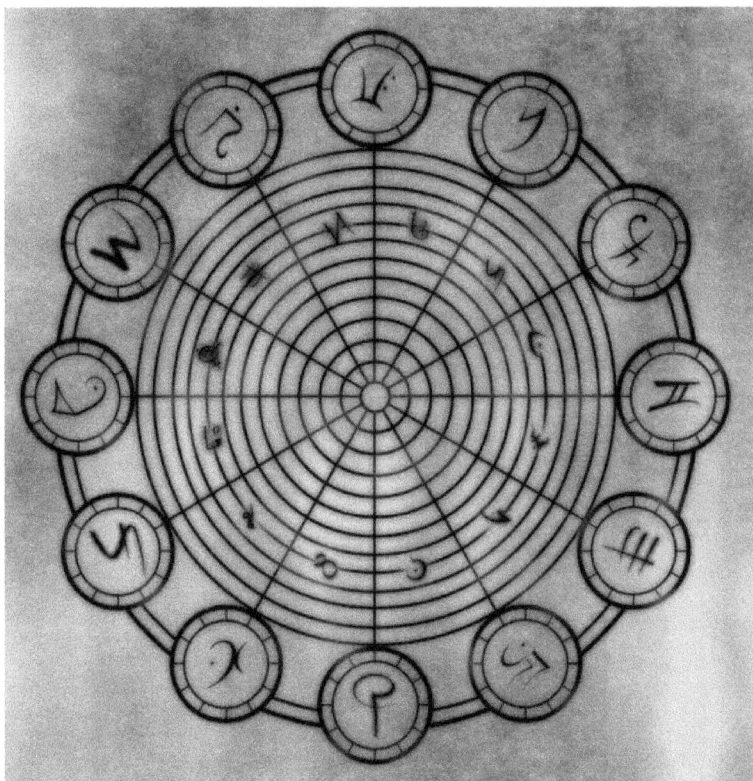

In this chapter, we'll discuss the meanings and interpretations of various runes under the Tyr's aett including Teiwaz, Berkana, Ehwaz, Mannaz, Laguz, and Inguz. You'll also see the runic symbol of each as well as its corresponding relations to the runic gods, zodiac sign, tarot card, planet, color, and polarity. As you now know, Tyr (Tir, Tiw, Teiwaz) is known as the god of war, and it's also the final aett set before the wyrd or blank rune (which we will discuss in the next chapter) which is something that's related with fate or karma and something that's outside the aetts.

Teiwaz

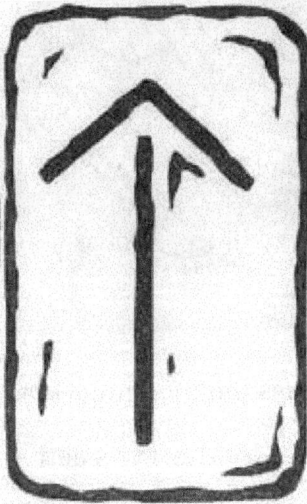

or

- God Relation: Tyr
- Nature Relation: Hazel & Oak Trees; Purple Sage
- Zodiac Sign: Virgo
- Tarot Link – Justice
- Colour – Flame Red
- Polarity – Male

- Anglo - Saxon runic poem in relation to Teiwaz: 'Tiw is a guiding star, well does it keep faith with princes: it is ever on its course over the mists of night and never fails.'

- Norwegian runic poem in relation to Teiwaz: 'Tyr is one-handed among the gods; oft has the smith to blow.'

- The Icelandic runic poem in relation to Teiwaz: 'Tyr is one-handed among the gods and leavings of wolf and king of temples.'

The rune of Teiwaz is linked to the god of the warriors – Tyr. Tyr is equivalent to the Roman god Mars. He is the predecessor of the Chief God Odin, and is regarded as the All – Father God of the Vikings.

Teiwaz is also known as the "rune of love" even if it's polarity is male, and is strongly linked with wars and battles. However, it can also represent selfishness in a relationship.

If the arrow of Teiwaz in the symbol is pointed downwards, it denotes that a person is in a superficial relationship which means that women shouldn't give their full trust to their men because the relationship is only temporary perhaps because the man is too demanding. On the other hand, if the symbol is pointing upwards, then that means that the relationship is guided by the gods, and that any obstacle that the lovers or couples will face can be overcome and the relationship could last. In line with this, if the rune is drawn pointing up and the questioner is a man, then that could mean he will strongly love a woman, while if the questioner is a woman, she will find a guy who is handsome, strong, and someone who will love her.

According to the rune masters, it's useful to meditate with the rune of Teiwaz in its upright position if a person seeks answers to certain problems.

In addition, success in entrepreneurial pursuits is very likely if the rune is drawn in an upright position. The person should seize opportunities and also be aware of his/her strength. Legal matters and anything relating to sports is also very favorable.

The rune of Teiwaz also denotes that one should undertake whatever project or opportunity comes with a sense of purpose and clear goals, not letting anyone or anything get in the way to achieving it.

Aside from that, this rune is also linked with physical attraction, leadership, justice, honor, invincibility and authority.

In Reverse

Just like what's mentioned earlier, if it's drawn in a reverse it has something to do with relationships but it can also mean some behavioral and health problems as well as problems concerning properties.

Berkana

BERKANA

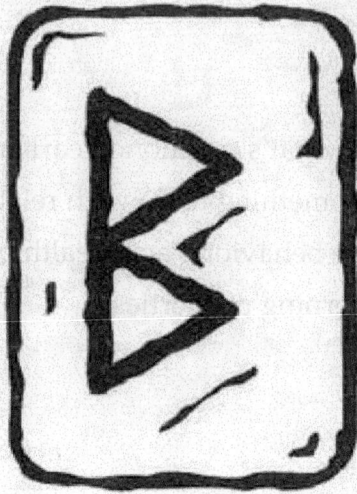

- Animal Relation: Bear; Swan
- God Relation: Nerthus
- Nature Relation: Fig trees; Birch tree; Herb Lady's Mantle
- Zodiac Sign: Cancer
- Tarot Link – Empress
- Colour – Green
- Polarity – Female

- Anglo - Saxon runic poem in relation to Berkana: 'Beorc bears no fruit, yet without seed it brings forth shoots, for it is generated from its leaves. Splendid are its branches and gloriously adorned, its lofty crown reaching the skies.'

- Norwegian runic poem in relation to Berkana: 'Bjarkan is greenest-leafed of branches; Loki was lucky in his deception.'

- The Icelandic runic poem in relation to Berkana: 'Bjarkan is leafy branch and little tree and youthful shrub.'

The rune of Berkana is connected with fertility and home – life. In astrology, Cancer is connected with the Moon and spirituality, while in Tarot reading, it is something related to one's intuition.

Therefore, this rune suggests that a person should look beyond material things, and pay attention to their spiritual being/ spiritual aspect. Sometimes we need to look at ourselves, and really try to connect with our inner being, and take the time to learn our true desires and goals in life. The rune suggests that one should also let go of things that doesn't make us happy, and reflect on our true motives in life.

Berkana also denotes that new projects will come along that can be a source of personal growth and develop one's relationship with their families. It's a time for new beginnings because it's also connected with starting a new family, having a new job, having a new baby, getting married etc. It denotes that there can be causes for celebration both within a person's family circle and outside of it.

Do keep in mind that anything new needs time, attention, and nurture so that it can grow to its fullest potential whether it is related to one's spiritual aspect, relationships, careers, or other important matters.

In Reverse

Berkana when drawn in reverse could mean that there's problems in growth perhaps because of wrong choices which is why it may be necessary for a person to pause and think about what they're doing so that they can start again. It can also suggests health concerns within the family, postponements of celebrations, and also feeling of disease.

Ehwaz

- Animal Relation: Horse
- God Relation: Freyja
- Nature Relation: Apple tree; Oak tree; Ash tree
- Planet: Mercury (positive aspect)
- Tarot Link – The Lovers
- Colour – White
- Polarity – Male/ Female

- Anglo - Saxon runic poem in relation to Ehwaz: 'Eh is a joy to princes in the presence of warriors, a steed in the pride of its hooves, when rich men discuss it, it is ever a comfort to the restless.'

The rune of Ehwaz is related to the status of a person and that of others. Drawing out this rune also denotes that new opportunities in the fields of science or higher education are very likely.

Changes will also happen on a large scale if Ehwaz is drawn which means that emotions can run high and it's something that a person should be careful with.

The animal connection is a horse which means that there would be some sort of travel or transfer, perhaps moving in to a new house/ location, or a strong partnership (both romantic and in business/legal matters).

Needless to say, things are changing for the better but one should still take precautions. There should be a sense of respect, trust and loyalty especially if it's denoting a new partnership because that's what's going to create a successful team.

The rune of Ehwaz is also strongly associated with the planet Mercury – which is known as the planet of communication. A person can meditate on this rune especially if one wants to assess their spiritual aspect; harmony and also control is essential if one wants to have a successful journey.

In Reverse

If the rune of Ehwaz is drawn in a reverse position, it could mean that there are problems in transportation, and certain journeys particularly at sea can be cancelled or delayed. Animals may also become sick.

Mannaz

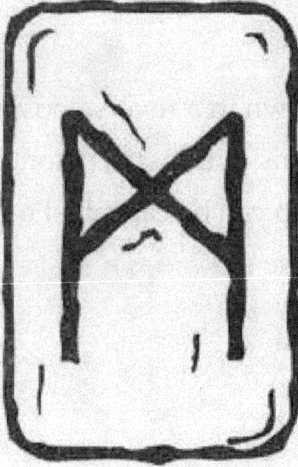 or

- Animal Relation: Hawk
- God Relation: Odin, Heimdall, Frigg
- Nature Relation: Ash tree; Elm tree; Maple; Madder Herb; Holly Bush
- Zodiac Sign: Aquarius
- Tarot Link – The Magician
- Colour – Red
- Polarity – Male/Female

- Anglo - Saxon runic poem in relation to Mannaz: 'Mann is a dear one to his kinsmen, yet each must fail his fellow, as the body is committed to the earth.'

- Norwegian runic poem in relation to Mannaz: 'Madr is augmentation of dust; great is the claw of the hawk.'

- The Icelandic runic poem in relation to Mannaz: 'Madr is the joy of man and augmentation of dust and adorner of ships.'

The rune of Mannaz relates to the inquirer, to oneself, and alto to correct personal behaviors. This rune is also linked to shared experiences, and is concerned with relationships both to oneself, and that of others. It also reminds us of our limited time on earth.

This rune also suggests that a person should look at the way they act towards other people and whenever they are alone or just by themselves.

It also denotes that a person should perhaps consult a professional before entering into anything, may it be business partnerships, relationships, new projects etc. This rune tells us to not act in haste, plan but not too far in the future. It tells us to look within ourselves a bit more and also see clearly the motives of other people.

This rune also suggests that one should watch their health. Legal matters and conflicts may also arise which is something that can stress the inquirer.

The New Age, other's welfare and the environment are going some things that will be interesting to you. The rune also means 'help.'

In Reverse

If the rune of Mannaz is drawn in a reverse position, then it could indicate some potential enemies, perhaps someone with authority, or also someone that's not from your own country/ culture.

This rune can be asked for help to avoid such potential conflicts and outside enemies but it's also important to look within oneself that could lead a person in doing the right thing.

Rune masters also suggest that the rune of Mannaz in a reverse position can relate to the subject's father who may be strict.

Laguz

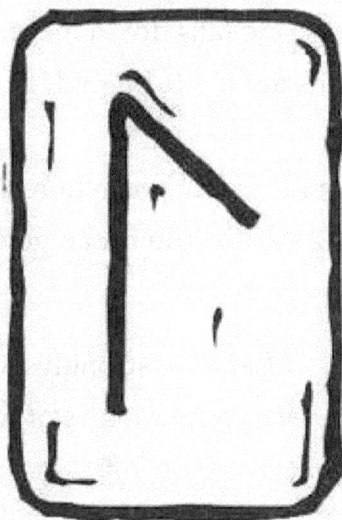

- Animal Relation: Seal; Gull
- God Relation: Njord
- Nature Relation: Willow tree; Osier tree; Water
- Planet - Moon
- Tarot Link – The Star
- Colour – Green
- Polarity – Female

- Anglo - Saxon runic poem in relation to Laguz: 'Lagu seems interminable to men if they venture on the rolling bark and the waves of the sea afright them and the courses of the deep heed not its bridle.'

- Norwegian runic poem in relation to Laguz: 'Logr is where cascade falls down mountain-side; but ornaments are made of gold.'

- The Icelandic runic poem in relation to Laguz: 'Logr is welling stream and broad geyser and land of fish.'

The rune of Laguz is strongly associated with water, and the sea as well as other bodies of water like waterfalls, and also sea shells.

This rune can denote that success and material things may be acquired or even lost, and it's something that's outside one's control.

Things may also likely to flow in a person's life if this rune is drawn, and just like the sea sometimes it can be kind, but when the storm comes, it can also seem harsh. Water is fluid but also strong. In general, water is something that humans can't live without, and also something that cannot be controlled. This is to remind us that success will come at its own time, and circumstances cannot be forced especially if the power lies with other people/ factors.

Aside from that, the rune is also linked with travel, perhaps it's something that is overseas, or concerned with personal/ business matters.

Imagination can run high when the rune of Laguz is drawn, and it's very likely of it suggesting that one needs to reinforce its interest in spiritual or psychic matters. A person may need to undergo some form of spiritual cleansing through using one's intuition.

The rune of Laguz also denotes fertility in women, and may signify pregnancy and children.

In Reverse

If the rune of Laguz is drawn in reverse, then one should stop trying too hard when things aren't working out or the way it's planned. One should also just stay within their limits, and not consume anything bad like too much alcohol or junk foods. A person should also watch out for their emotions and not be too sensitive or dependent on what other people will say. The rune of Laguz in reverse is simply suggesting that one should also use their logic when making decisions.

Inguz

INGUZ

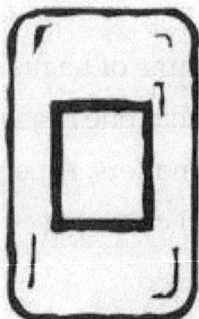

This is also sometimes seen as

- Animal Relation: Boar; Cuckoo
- God Relation: Ing
- Nature Relation: Laurel; Rosemary; Moon
- Planet – Venus (positive phase)
- Tarot Link – Judgement
- Colour – Yellow
- Polarity – Male/Female

- Anglo - Saxon runic poem in relation to Inguz: 'Ing was amongst the East-Danes first seen by men, till later east he went over the wave; his wain followed after; the Headings named the hero so.'

According to rune masters, the rune of Inguz is the doorway to the astral world, and is strongly linked with the apple tree, and the herb self – heal.

It is also linked with the health and fertility among males, and may denote of a new baby, creative energy, and contact with close relatives.

It's also very likely that one will move or get a new job, and change is coming. Problems may be resolved at this point, or it will take on a new path. It indicates that a new opportunity will come, and there'll be a burst of energy once a new project is undertaken. However, it also calls for a person to practice some patience as such things can take time, whilst, it's wise to take the time to have a clear mindset about certain things.

The rune of Inguz can also mean that a relationship will end because it's going nowhere; it may also suggest that one will take on a new interest or project. Holidays will be very likely once this rune is drawn, and relaxation is favored.

In Reverse

According to rune masters, there's no meaning if the rune of Inguz is drawn in reverse but for some it may mean some form of tension, stress, lack of progress, restrictions and frustrations to a person.

Chapter Seven: The Blank Runes and Rune Casting

Now that we have covered some of the major symbols in different aetts, and have learned their possible interpretations and meanings in detail, the next thing to learn is the rune that has no symbols but definitely with a strong meaning, such runes are known as wyrd or blank rune. Aside from the blank runes, this chapter will also cover how you can create a new name using the different rune, and what kind should you go before and after the name so that it can resonate well with the intentions of the holder. You'll also learn how to cast runes, and the runic Kabbala.

Wyrd or Blank Rune

The Blank Runes have no associations with animals, nature, planets, signs, and zodiac compared to the runes found in Frey'r, Haegl's, and Tyr's Aetts. As mentioned in the previous chapter, the wyrd rune is something that's related to karma and one's fate. It's concerned with things that cannot be predicted or avoided. The wyrd runes contain no symbol, and have no place in the alphabetical system because it's only purpose is to be casted out.

Wyrd is a word from the Anglo – Saxons; it's also related to a Viking word called Orlog which means fate, doom, and destiny.

The blank rune is also strongly linked with chief god Odin because the Vikings look up to him as the almighty god, the one with whom the Vikings can entrust their lives but also something that instills fear in them.

Karma came from an Indian word that simply means destiny or something that's related to fate. For the Hindus, we humans are already given a book where each of our life stories is already outlined but it's up to us to fill the rest of the story through our choices and free will.

The story's outline is what is meant by fate or karma, and this ideology is usually linked with our past lives – the way we acted, we behaved, and how we can right our own wrongs so that we can learn and progress. To some people, karma is the law of cause and effect but it sometimes can cause a wrong assumption that it's a punishment for past misbehaviors or wrong actions. Karma should be looked at as an opportunity to make up for the wrong things we have done in the present lifetime, the next or our past lives.

You have to keep in mind that there are things outside your control and that such things can happen where it will leave us no choice but to put it up to fate. This is what Karma is all about.

It's a pre - destined path that awaits us all – and this is what the blank runes are telling us. However, there are still things that we can control despite of whatever circumstances we are in. We have the power to control our reactions, and we always have a choice, not choosing to act *is* a choice. This is what the wyrd runes are trying to teach us – to do what we can and to the best of our ability but to also leave the rest of what we cannot control to fate.

According to rune masters, the only way to get out of the karmic chain is by learning how to forgive or what they call the Law of Grace.

You see, every action we do creates a sort of karmic progression wherein one can ease matters and learn. Drawing out wyrd runes may suggest that one should, at some degree let the universe or a higher force take care of some things for us, and it encourages us to trust the process, and believe that everything will fall into place at the right time.

It denotes that one should trust the universe especially when it comes to things we do not know, we do not understand, and the things we remain fearful about. Fate will determine your destiny only if you let it, but it's also important to keep in mind that sometimes you can only get out of a situation if you really tried your best, and leave the rest. Karma in general is an opportunity for a person to make themselves better. "Bad karma" only happens because of lack of love, negative outlook, fear, and also lack of wisdom.

The Wyrd Rune in a Casting

If the blank rune is drawn, it can denote that a major change will happen, or a questionnaire's life will have some sort of turning point.

It can also signify death – death of a circumstance and not merely a form of loss of a loved one or physical death. As you may know, it's sometimes necessary that one situation should end in order to give way for new beginnings. We should just have faith that whatever will come will ultimately be better and good for us or at the very least, gives us a chance to learn and become a better person. It may also denote that one should consider letting go of bad personalities or death of self – image. Do remember that powerful forces are in control and we as mere humans are subject to it which is why change and adaptability is necessary if we want to survive and thrive.

The wyrd rune is regarded by the Vikings as something powerful since it is related to the chief god who dictate's one's fate.

Changing Name Based on Runic Symbols

Before you learn how to lay out the runes for guidance, we'll first teach you how you can use the runes to change your name, and perhaps attract luck by etching it out in amulets or jewelry that you can wear every day. Below are the runic symbols that are equivalent to the English alphabet. Do keep in mind that the alphabetical links discussed in previous chapters are not tallied with this one.

A	B	C	D	E	F	G	H	I	J	K	L	M
ᚠ	ᛒ	ᚲ	ᛩ	ᛖ	ᚴ	ᚷ	ᚺ	ᛁ	ᛋ	ᚲ	ᚱ	ᛘ

N	O	P	Q	R	S	T	U	V	W	X	Y	Z
ᚾ	ᚢ	ᛈ	ᚲ	ᚱ	ᛋ	ᛏ	ᚢ	ᚠ	ᛝ	ᛉ	ᛁ	ᛁ

For those of you who understand numerology, and how various energies can influence a person's direction in life can relate to the idea of changing names to create a better life situation or to avoid any sort of hindrance or delay in future progress.

Say for example, you're a writer, and you're looking for a name of a character, and the name you chose is Brenda Shaw. Using the table below, you can come up with the appropriate runic symbols. But before you do that, you must first decide which runes should go before the name (leaders), and also after it (sealers) so that it is enclosed in a form of protective element.

The table given below will show you how each rune is use for specific purposes; such things/ meanings must not be changed and it should be exactly followed for it to be very effective. Give it a try and see if it works for you.

	THE LEADER	THE SEALER
MUSIC		
THE ARTS		
MYSTICISM		
MAGIC		
TRAVEL		
HOME		
STUDY		
LAW		
MEDICINE /HEALTH		

PARENThOOD	ᛒ	ᛝ
MECHANICAL THINGS	ᛚ	ᛏ
SCIENCE	ᚾ	ᛦ
TEACHING	ᛞ	ᚠ
WRITING	ᛗ	ᚱ
FARMING	◇	ᛋ

Runic Kabbala

Kabbala is a word that means "secret" or "hidden," and it is quite popular because it's also being used in other magical systems, and alternative religion. It's also quite interesting that Kabbala is also strongly linked with the art of runes, and it's also connected with the Kabbalistic Tree of Life which in runic is known as Yggdrasil or World Ash Tree. Based on tradition, the Tree of Life contains the whole of creation which is also known as the Nine Worlds.

According to rune masters the Kabbala and the original meanings of runes were never written down and were only handed to students through word of their mouth. Those who are students of Kabbala known that the Tree of Life has 22 paths that runs in 10 sephiroths or stations. Such sephiroths are connected with various things which is also shown in the figure below but it's also important to note that one should understand fully what each of these paths mean so that you can properly and strongly meditate on it, and also associate it with the appropriate runic symbols.

What is Kabbala?

Kabbala is mainly concerned with the creation of the world. According to this principle, God created the world through the 32 secret paths of wisdom; 10 of which is known as the Sephiroths, and the rest is the 22 letters in the Hebrew alphabet.

Each path in the 10 sephiroths is like a level of knowledge that one needs to be attained; and the lower 7 corresponds to the Chakras of the body or the main energy points in the body. The Sephiroths are also known to compromise God's name which is Yahweh.

Kabbala masters suggest that it's very possible to achieve spiritual awakening if one learns how to meditate in the Kabbalistic Tree of Life, the same way people meditate when they're going to a yoga classes.

Using the Sephiroths discussed in this section as well as the runes linked to it will definitely increase spiritual awareness, and perhaps raise consciousness.

Reflecting the Sephiroth should be the main focus in the beginning but then it should also draw from certain experiences gained.

Some Kabbalist practitioner also uses colors and sound whenever they are meditating on the 10 sephiroths while other connect them planets, Chakra centers of the body, angels, numbers, angels and metals. You'll get better with experience. The basic meanings of the Kabbalistic Tree of Life are given below:

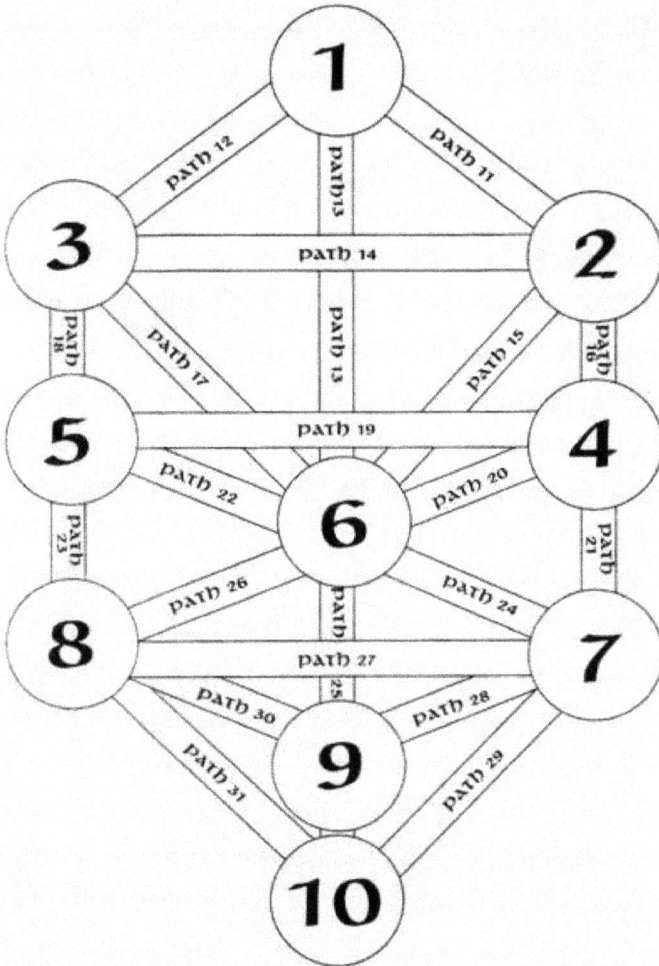

- Kether - crown
- Chokmah - wisdom
- Binah - understanding
- Chesed - mercy
- Geburah - severity
- Tiphareth - beauty
- Netzach - victory
- Hod - glory

- Yesod - foundation
- Malkuth – kingdom

The 24 runes will fit within this plan; Sephiroths 11 and 12 are also assigned to 2 runes each, one in ascending, and the other one is in descending which is why the 24 runes will fit (ignore the blank runes for now).

Bind Runes

Bind runes are 2 runes that are combined together to form a symbol. Bind runes are usually used on jewelry and worn as an amulet so that the person can wear it whenever he/she wants to.

If you want to come up with your own bind runes, you can check out the illustration below to get some ideas on how to do it, it'll definitely be an fascinating experience because it's like you're coming up with your own fusion of symbols that will bring you good luck or positive energy. You can also customize bind runes for someone and give it to them as a gift or souvenir.

GOOD LUCK

HAPPY MARRIAGE

SUCCESS IN LEGAL ACTION

POWER

PROBLEMS WITH CONCEPTION

MENTAL POWER

LOVE (MAN FOR WOMAN)

LOVE (WOMAN FOR MAN)

Different Ways in Casting Runes

There are various ways on how you can lay runes for casting. What we will show you in this chapter is only some of the most common way; you can research different ways on your own as there are perhaps a hundred ways to cast a rune.

What you can do is to try the ways that will be illustrated here, and see for yourself if it's something that resonates with you or something that will feel comfortable. The important thing is that you are familiar with the meanings of the runes, their connections to one another, and how they are read as a group before you can progress to more advance methods which you will learn through further research and practice.

Do keep in mind that even if the meanings of each rune are given in previous chapters, it's still important that you don't dismiss any personal or intuitive thoughts that you will have whenever you're doing a runic reading or at the time you're carrying out the casting. The things we've listed in this book cover only the basics which are suitable for beginners. There are a lot more runes to study about and perhaps a much deeper meaning that we were not able to cover in this book, which is why it's important that you research on your own and read other related references if this is something that you wish to master.

As always, it will take time before you can master practically anything in life which is why patience and constant practice is key in order for you to become better at practicing this art. Experience is the best teacher so keep trying and keep learning more about this craft because that's how you're going to formulate your own personal interpretations and make you more accurate in your runic readings.

The Rune Master's Way

In previous chapters, we mentioned that rune masters usually draw 3 sets of 3 runes because it indicates the past, present, and future. The runes are cast in this way, and are laid from right to left as shown in the illustration below:

Odin's Casting

Another common way of casting runes is by laying 5 runes from right to left; this is known as Odin's Casting. The 3rd rune is slightly raised from the other runes. This kind of casting or laying is also used in Tarot card readings.

| 5 | 4 | 3 | 2 | 1 |

Similar layout can also be applied with 7 runes, and even 12 runes. The 12 runes can be associated with the months or the zodiac signs since it can represent an entire year. As shown in the figure on the next page, it's commonly laid out in a circle form. However, there are also variations of this type of layout.

```
        1   12
    2             11
  3                 10
  4                 9
    5             8
        6   7
```

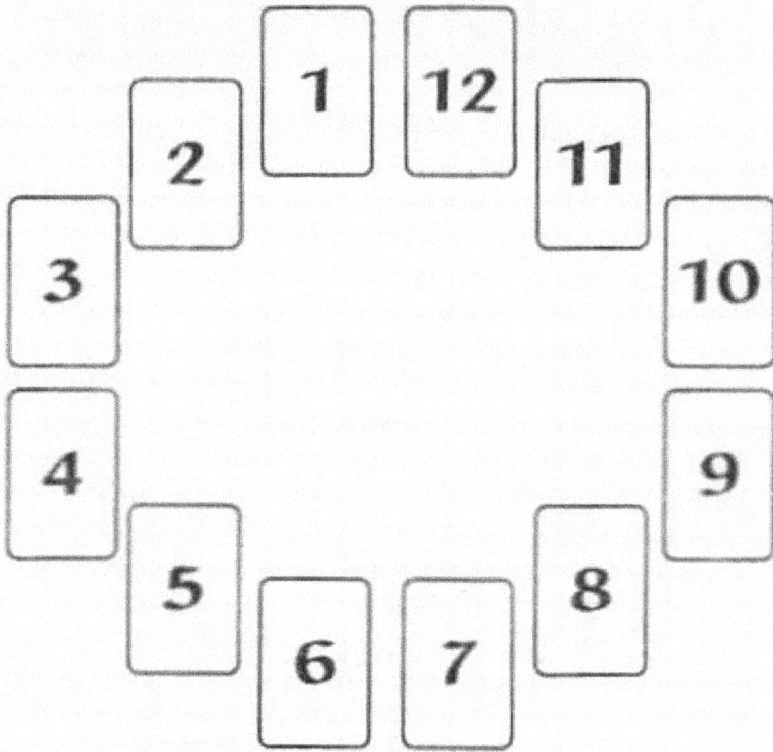

The Runic Cross

One of the most popular ways of casting out runes is known as the Runic Cross which is illustrated in the figure below. According to many runic readers, for some reason, this kind of layout can be quite rewarding.

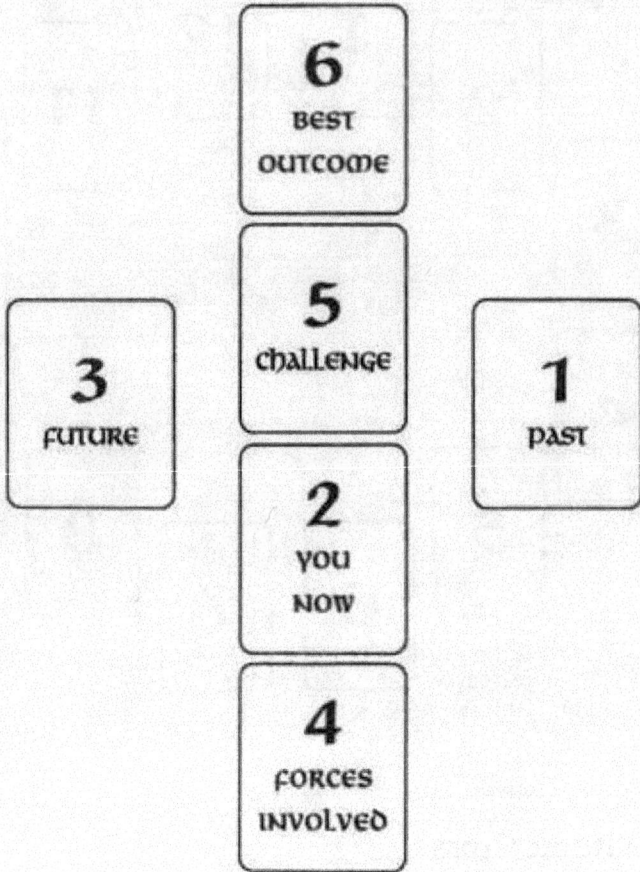

Chapter Eight: Conclusion and Samples of Runic Reading

In this chapter we will help you get started and also guide you on how you can practically cast the runes and apply some of the basic things and concepts you've learned in this book. Some of the answers will be given to you as a guide but there will be situations where we won't. Do keep in mind that when it comes to practicing the casting of runes there's no standard way or set rules of helping other people or even yourself. Therefore, it's important that you are open when it comes to interpreting what the runes might be telling you, and most of the time this ability will be develop through constant practice and experience. There's no right or wrong, and the answers to whatever question you have may or may not be always accurate but practice can get you closer to the truth of whatever you or your subjects would like to know.

Let's Start the Exercise!

In order to help you apply what you've learned so far, and for you to have a realistic idea of how the art of runes works, we'll pretend that you're doing a casting for a particular subject, say your friend at the office or your colleague. Here's the characteristics and situation of your friend:

She is a middle – aged mom who has 2 children; a son and a daughter. Her children are already grown-ups and already have their own families. At the moment she feels that she's sort of stuck in her life, and thinks that she isn't capable enough of doing certain things like getting that promotion because of her age. She's kind of wondering whether or not she should just take a job offer in another company for a totally different field and left her current work where she spent the last 20 years.

What you do now to help her is to use different ways of casting the runes. Your work mate chose to use the 5 – rune casting method which was discussed in previous chapters. From your pouch, the runes that she drew were the following (in order):

- Perth
- Teiwaz
- Nauthiz
- Jera
- Fehu

The runes are laid from right to the left, and let's just say that all of it is the right way up. The question now is, how would you choose to interpret the meanings of the runes taking into account your friend's current situation, and her inquiry?

Do keep in mind the keywords to each of the rune she chose. You should also make sure to look at the runes laid out individually and collectively. If you remember, Nauthiz rune which is the 3rd rune may represent the thing that's stopping changes or movement but how does this relate to its actual meaning? Does this mean that your friend should give up on her plans? What you can do then is to take a look at the next 2 runes to create a conclusion.

What you can do is to write down the runes, its meanings or representations, and write down your initial answer. However, if you're the intuitive kind, perhaps you can form an interpretation without jotting it down.

So let's just say you have made an interpretation but your friend still isn't sure of what to do. She then decide to get one more run to answer her question in the form of 'yes' or 'no.' Ideally, the question should go like this; "Should I stay in the job I'm in now?" Let's say that the rune she picked is the Uruz and it's in an upright position. What you can do now is to think the animal that the rune represents or think of the keywords, and anything that may be associated with it while keeping in mind your friend's inquiry and situation. How will you now interpret it? The answer will eventually come out but it's not easy and of course not definite. In addition, what if the Uruz is drawn in an inverted position? It can totally have a different meaning right?

Practicing with Sigils

In this section, the exercise will give you a chance to practice the art of rune in the form of sigils or the rune word.

Let's say you go to a craft fair, and you met someone who's a jewelry maker. You then explained to her that you have an interest in runic alphabet or symbolism and that you would like your name etched in a necklace using the runic symbols. Let's say your name is Karan (Hint: Take note of the spelling). You are a secretary and have recently got a call to an audition for a possible contract signing. If you make it in this audition, it could definitely lead you to becoming famous or lead you to other bigger opportunities, which is why you need as much help once you go in.

You look at the runes available, and you need to decide which ones you should use. Do keep in mind that there's different links when it comes to the runic symbols and corresponding English alphabet that will get your name right. What kind of leader rune would you want to use before your name? What would be the sealer rune?

We will suggest that you get Laguz, Kaunuz, Ansuz, Raido, Ansuz, Nauthiz and Gebo in that order. Is it wrong or right? Make sure to practice in drawing the symbols that each rune represents. Would you consider changing your name when it's translated in runes? It's advisable that you also consider looking at numerological links before you choose what kind of name you want to be etched in your necklace. This is where your training will come in. It's all up to you.

Runes for Healing Exercise

Now let's do another exercise wherein we will still use the rune words or sigils but this time it's for healing purposes.

The situation is this; a woman named Sara suffers from headaches. According to her doctor, it's all because of tension and stress. You as a friend, would like to help her calm down to ease the pain she feels physically. Among other things, you want to help her by using runes. What then would you suggest that she choose to help her?

Do you think Algiz is appropriate? Would you advise her to meditate on this rune because it's the one that is linked with headaches? Do you think meditation will calm her down? What if she hasn't meditated before and doesn't know how to do it?

You then decide to give her jewelry with a healing sigil etched in it. You have the option of putting one for the physical and one for the emotional aspect. Which one should you choose? And can you only choose one or both? There isn't a clear answer but once you get a feel of how to do things using the runes, it'll get much easier as you practice using it often.

Just a Precaution

Before this book comes to an end, it's also important to note that using runes can also cause problems, and this can happen if you don't fully understand the concept of this art, and don't have any clue of what you're doing.

A Nordic saga has this story where a young guy who got a hold of a runic sigil on the piece of whalebone attempted to use it and try to heal a young girl. When he gave the whalebone, the girl became rather worse. Another young man by the name of Egil, which is a great poet and also warrior, removed the runic sigil from the whalebone and burned it. He then replaced it with the correct symbols, and eventually the sick girl became better.

Now, this may not be significant in our modern lives but it can serve the importance of getting things right. Giving a wrong interpretation or advising things that you aren't sure of because you don't fully understand how it works yet can be damaging to yourself and also to the lives of your subjects in the same way that the girl's condition got worse because of using the wrong sigils.

Make sure that before you cast runes, you have fully grasped the concepts, meaning, and principles behind this ancient art through knowledge and also practice. What you say and how you say things can definitely impact your subject whom you will help. You should also not force casting runes on anyone especially if they don't feel comfortable doing it. If you do wish to help, you can ask their permission and explain to them this ancient art. You can also draw a rune to help you decide whether or not you should do runic reading for a particular person. If the answer is No then so be it, don't force it.

If you wanted to write a runic symbol, then make sure that it makes sense, and that you're already quite knowledgeable on how to do it. Perhaps, ask a rune master to help you and see if you already have what it takes. Otherwise, it's best left to those people who have studied it in great detail. And since this book only covers the basics, it's best if you research about it and really take the time to learn before trying to do it on other people.

Messing with the art of runes may unleash things that could be difficult to deal with and also dangerous. As we've mentioned in the first chapter of this book, it should be treated with respect for it has magical purposes.

If you learn how to do it right it can help you make your life better and use it as a guiding principle in your everyday life just like how the Vikings use it to their advantage. It can be worthwhile to learn but it will definitely take your time and teach you about patience. We suggest that if you're interested in continuing your journey through this art form, and possibly want to become a rune master, then further study of the symbolisms, history, runic poetry and all its meanings is a must. Joining a group where the casting of rune is being studies is also great so that others can help you in your self – discovery and enlightenment of the physical and spiritual world.

Photo Credits

References

A Beginner's Guide: Runes – Krystyna Arcati
https://coreyemmah.weebly.com/uploads/2/2/1/8/22181700/runes.pdf

Runes – Wikipedia.org
https://en.wikipedia.org/wiki/Runes

Runes – Norse – Mythology.org
https://norse-mythology.org/runes/

The Origins of the Runes – Norse – Mythology.org

https://norse-mythology.org/runes/the-origins-of-the-runes/

Runic Philosophy and Magic – Norse – Mythology.org

https://norse-mythology.org/runes/runic-philosophy-and-magic/

The Meanings of the Runes – Norse – Mythology.org

https://norse-mythology.org/runes/the-meanings-of-the-runes/

What Are Runes? – HolisticShop UK

https://www.holisticshop.co.uk/articles/guide-runes

Runes, Alphabet of Mystery – Sunnyway.com

http://sunnyway.com/runes/

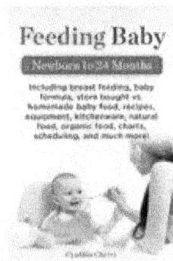

Feeding Baby
Cynthia Cherry
978-1941070000

Axolotl
Lolly Brown
978-0989658430

Dysautonomia, POTS
Syndrome
Frederick Earlstein
978-0989658485

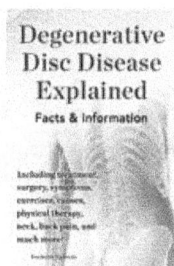

Degenerative Disc
Disease Explained
Frederick Earlstein
978-0989658485

Sinusitis, Hay Fever,
Allergic Rhinitis Explained
Frederick Earlstein
978-1941070024

Wicca
Riley Star
978-1941070130

Zombie Apocalypse
Rex Cutty
978-1941070154

Capybara
Lolly Brown
978-1941070062

Eels As Pets
Lolly Brown
978-1941070167

Scabies and Lice Explained
Frederick Earlstein
978-1941070017

Saltwater Fish As Pets
Lolly Brown
978-0989658461

Torticollis Explained
Frederick Earlstein
978-1941070055

Kennel Cough
Lolly Brown
978-0989658409

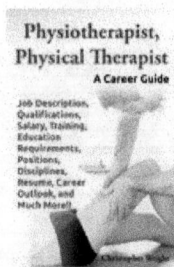

Physiotherapist, Physical
Therapist
Christopher Wright
978-0989658492

Rats, Mice, and Dormice
As Pets
Lolly Brown
978-1941070079

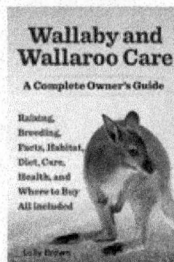

Wallaby and Wallaroo Care
Lolly Brown
978-1941070031

Bodybuilding Supplements
Explained
Jon Shelton
978-1941070239

Demonology
Riley Star
978-19401070314

Pigeon Racing
Lolly Brown
978-1941070307

Dwarf Hamster
Lolly Brown
978-1941070390

Cryptozoology
Rex Cutty
978-1941070406

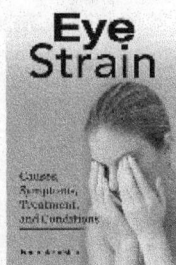

Eye Strain
Frederick Earlstein
978-1941070369

Inez The Miniature Elephant
Asher Ray
978-1941070353

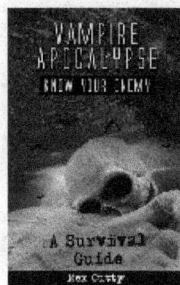

Vampire Apocalypse
Rex Cutty
978-1941070321